He was a Good Father

Mark Borczon

Nixes Mate Books
Allston, Massachusetts

Copyright © 2017 Mark Borczon

Book design by d'Entremont
Front cover snapshot from the collection of Lauren Leja

All rights reserved. This book or any portion thereof may not be reproduced or used in any manner whatsoever without the express written permission of the publisher except for the use of brief quotations in a book review or scholarly journal.

Thanks and love to Janice Felix, Lily, Aurora and Sophia Borczon, Lonnie Sherman, Geoff Peterson and Matthew Borczon.

ISBN 978-0-9993971-1-4

Nixes Mate Books
POBox 1179
Allston, MA 02134
nixesmate.pub/books

"When Death beats his children no one listens"
  – Frank Stanford

This book is dedicated to the memory of my father,
Arthur Felix Borczon

Contents

He Was A Good Father	1
The Night Watchman	2
I Am Dreaming I Am Still Alive	3
Catholic Cemetery Road	4
A Blind Horse	7
Between Death And A Drowning Man	8
Leave A Shadow	10
Mushrooms	12
Good Night, Baby, Daddy's Time Ain't Long	15
Feeding Vodka To A Wicked Frenchman's Muse	16
Burial	18
The Place Where The Crow Went Blind	20
Baudelaire	22
The New Girlfriend	23

When I Hit The Road	24
This Is Not A Poem About My Job,	
This Is A Poem About Work	26
I Stand On The Corner	30
Amen	32
Railroad Boots Beside The Bed	34
Dress Rehearsal	37
Coyote In Workboots	38
When John Henry Went To College	41
Ink Stained Ghost	45
Bottom Shelf Vodka And A Love	
That Will Last Forever	47

He was a Good Father

He Was A Good Father

He kept the handgun
In the night stand
And the bullets
In the sock drawer

He kept his vodka
In the ice box
And his children
In the dark

The Night Watchman

I hold my tongue
With both hands
And keep an ice pick
Tucked in my boot
I take my days
Like a bath
In a shallow grave
When I walk
My steps are so heavy
The moon is shook
From the sky
I load my rifle
With rock salt
And knuckle bones
If I find you
In my orchard
At night
You will die
Like somebody
In the Bible

I Am Dreaming I Am Still Alive

When it's time to ply his trade
Death sends a clown in hobo rags
Carrying a flower that
You should refuse to sniff

Me and life have spent years
Like two horses standing on a hill
Facing opposite directions

At best we each tolerate
The other's smell
At worst we've never met

Catholic Cemetery Road

The dead deer along
The side of the road
Look like cloistered monks
Lamp less in the weeds
Like hands folded
In prayer
Like my daughters
Sleeping
Like the consequences
Of an unprincipled
God

The spectral night along
Catholic Cemetery road
Calls for a spotlight
And a 30-30
On the passenger side
Barren trees drive
The conversation
Using a tombstone
For a tongue

I search the gullies
And up the low rise

For a wounded pony
Lost with his misery
Needing settled
The sound of
Dripping blood
Splashing
On dry leaves

I need this
Like I need my
Own name
Driving deep into
The county
Hunting for places
I have never been

Shoot the pony
Hear it fall
And feel its weight
Lift off my chest
Like a winter quilt
Then drive slowly
Spotting for deer
Because the tow

Would be expensive
And long
From where I was hit
To where
I fell

A Blind Horse
For Lonnie

The sun is a Chinese rooster
Singing the song of itself
At the top of it's voice
Rolling across the sky
Like a fist with
Two missing fingers

After fifty one years
Of working for a living
I have become a blind horse
Yoked to a mill stone
Circling endlessly, grinding
My endurance like wheat

The light in the sky
Means nothing to my eyes
And the warmth on my face
Is bathed in sweat
As I follow the carrot
I only remember
Having seen

Between Death And A Drowning Man

Desire is fat and shirtless
With pale, lunar spiders
Spinning chest hair into silk
Crocheting a heart knotted
In a dream catcher
Dangling from a canopy bed
Like a lynched convict
Left in moonlight

Hunger was the face
Eating her once beautiful face
Draining herself with vikadin
Like a hummingbird drinking
Water from the eye socket
Of a sugar skull
Hovering above
A sullen grave

We had our grandparent's poverty
Begging us to butcher
The Chinese rooster
And boil it in water
Collecting in a hole in the ground

Our love was a grave we shared
Called middle age
And I really did love you once
Like the breath that
Lay between death and
A drowning man
I would have
Traded anything
For you

Except myself
I lost too much of that
Just finding you
And I didn't have
Enough left
To keep you

Leave A Shadow

Tonight I dined on Kim chi pork
And lo-mien noodles
Then washed down the night medication
With vodka and strawberry lemonade

Sitting in bed with a copy
Of Lorca's Poet in New York
I notice the likeness between
Federico's passport photo
And pictures of Kafka
Living in Prague

I listen to the spiders singing
From the blades of the ceiling fan
Above the bed and think about
The tragic death of
Sam Cooke

Nothing to say about
The hours that led me here
Sitting in front of the TV.
Nose to nose with
My own meaninglessness

I have this one thought
If I wasn't a poet
I wouldn't leave
A shadow
In this town

Mushrooms
For Jason Baldinger

Back when I was seventeen
Me and my twin brother
And my cousin Bob were
Eating handfuls of dried mushrooms
Out of an army surplus knapsack
Waiting for the sky to
Call us by name
When a boy on a ten speed
Came down the hill dressed
In serious bicycling gear
He was as slick and blue black
As a pilot whale with
An enormous helmet
On his head
He was calling out
My name, said he wanted
To meet me because
I had just taken his
Girlfriend away from him
And he needed to look me
In the eye

I figured it was
Just the mushrooms
The song they played
Plucking the banjos
Behind my eyes
Not anything real
Just a pilot whale
Tucking his tail between
His legs, biking
Slowly back up the hill
And beaching himself
On a picnic table
On the edge of
The playground
To weep

This is how I learned
She had left him
She showed up an hour later
And was furious when
I told her he had come
And stole her thunder
Her anger was Shakespearian

When she discovered that
I already knew
She was mine

But I still thought
It was the mushrooms
Playing bird song on
The plastic harmonicas
Laying around my heart

That was thirty four
Years ago
She is a librarian
In Texas now
The pilot whale
Is a local weatherman
On the six o'clock news
And I am middle aged
Over weight and still
Convinced it was
The mushrooms
Re-arranging the bookshelves
In my memories
Of a bedroom
That was
Never mine

Good Night, Baby, Daddy's Time Ain't Long
For Lily, Aurora and Sophia

Starlight and rain are two things
You can't always get when you want them
They are identical with the
Terms of their arrival
And wanting can not influence
Their availability

Many things are like that
A meal when you're poor is like that
A cold beer at work is like that
A meaningful life is like that

You start wishing away time and you start
Dying faster, chasing the moment
Overtop the living you've paved flat
To get to that first drop of rain
That first shimmer of light, to breathe
It in as that most special breath
You've taken in a week
Not one breath longer or deeper
Than any other you've taken
Just the one full of
Starlight and rain

Feeding Vodka To A Wicked Frenchman's Muse

My heart is a calcified
Skeletal fist with
A hummingbird trapped
Inside of it

It is a gypsy midget
Taking tickets
At a side show

My heart is a phone booth
On a street corner
In Detroit, ringing unanswered
In an abandoned neighborhood

It is a good horse
With a broken leg
Staring at a shot gun

My heart is a violin
Passed through the window
Of an overcrowded
Train car

It is a pair of hands
Needing to be free
To scratch lice

My heart is the
Defiant sneer
On my father's
Plaster death mask

It is my mother
Sleeping alone
In a single bed

My heart is this poem
Written on my shadow
Getting taller, walking
Away from the light

It is the light
The dead see
And are drawn to

Burial

They brought his coffin
To the graveyard
In a wagon drawn by
A blind, white horse
One that couldn't be spooked
By all the cottonmouths

His grave was
A dangerous place
For those who
Loved him

It rained as they
Lowered him down
Then everyone
Left quickly

The hole took weeks
To fill with
Water

The grass beneath
The pile of dirt
Died

His coffin
Slowly buoyed
To the surface
Lifted by
Rain water

He was still
With them
In spite of
Their best
Efforts

To let
Him
Go

The Place Where The Crow Went Blind

"What will they say about my poetry?
Who never touched my blood?"
                              Neruda

She told me she loved me
And took me to the place
Where the crow went blind

I found two black feathers
Put one under my chin
And drew the other across it
Like a violin bow

It played a silence
In which I could hear
The music of her love

The universe is where
I found myself, oblivion
And me undifferentiated
Like winter and Christmas

Grace, walking with a limp
Striking by standards
With his cane
Without apology

I went back to that place
Looking for my lost watch
And death had soiled the nest
We made together

The air was without song
The feathers were burning
And death warmed his hands

But the memory of her love
Drew my body back home
From the place where
The crow went blind

Baudelaire

Something Baudelaire tried to say
To let the wine speak
Is to be free from the bonds of wounds

I was sober all but 6 months
Of the 12 years we were married
She liked her men
Wounded and
Silent

So did Baudelaire's

Poets like torture
That's why we attempt
To mate for life

That's why
We fail

The New Girlfriend

The far off lightning
Laces through the clouds
Touches down on water
And lights the bay

White teeth break a smile
Under tired eyes
The beautiful way
She asks me to leave

When I Hit The Road

I wanted to be
Blessed
I wanted to be
The wealthiest
Gypsy on the road
With the moon
And three Spanish
Guitars

I wanted rum
To puddle in the
Wheel ruts
Instead of
Yesterdays
Rain

What I got was
A one bedroom apartment
In a rust belt town
A third shift job
And a map to every
Dive bar that opens
At seven am.

My ex-wife
Took the kids
And the friends
I got to keep
That exquisite
First kiss

And all the lies
That came
After

Not too much
To carry
When I hit
The road

This Is Not A Poem About My Job, This Is A Poem About Work

It's a story
As old as work
Itself
The bad nights
The co-workers who
Labor harder to
Do nothing than
The actual doing
Of the job would
Require
The dull eyes
Of young workers
Who stare at their
Cell phones
Pretending they aren't
Even there
The frequent soliloquies
That always starts out
"I'm the only one
Who ever does anything
Around here"
The bitterness of
Stupid, little lives

Finding my profession
To be the hook
They hang it all
On

I have been doing this
For almost 30 years
Joined my union in 95
And have only just
Gotten by
But there was a time
When I thought
There was more for me
Than manual labor
Arthritis and
A creeping alcoholism
That found its
Magnetic other pole
In death

I had a fine mind
I got an education and
Even convinced

A few people that
I was worthy
Bought into it
Myself for
Longer than
I care to admit

And I wasn't always
As good as I am
Now
I was as much
A part of the problem
As I am now a
Part of the status quo

The best years of my life
Are gone and
The best years of my life
Sucked

So, right now
I am awake
At 12 o'clock in
The morning
Drinking vodka and
Ginger ale
After a mandated

Shift on my
Night off
Tired and
In pain
And pissed off
That my best effort
Couldn't fix anything
At the job
In the country
In the world
In the way
Things are

Please note
That I haven't
Told you
What I actually
Do to make
A living
 I don't think
I need to
In order for
You to
Get this

I Stand On The Corner

Tonight the fog over the bay
Could house Chinese hermits
While they search for enlightenment

Cold rain, falling like a shroud
Tossed off the roof of
An ancient cathedral

Twists in the air and coils
Like a kite tail that
Falls at my feet

I stand at the place
Where the blood
Meets the city

I stand where I have always
Been, dressed like Mingus
On eviction day

I stand on a corner
Smoking medical marijuana
With God

With the holy men
With the fog
And the rain

I stand
On the
Corner

Amen

Dull days are spent in cars
Or smelling burning cat hair
In the ashtray
A jar full of red wine
And the inane chatter
Bleeding from the TV.

That we crawled from the
Ancient oceans of earth
Into millions of years spent
Evolving just to get to this

Making wealthy men rich
While blaming ourselves
For not being one
Of them

Working so desperately
To get to eat, drink
Fuck, shit and piss
While hating ourselves
Over what we can't
Buy

Going mad or taking pills
Wishing for more time
Willing to take less living
For it

Dreaming the psychological
Nightmares we studied
In college – running down
A dark, wet street
Chased by a giant tit
Wielding a knife

Joining churches, reading
Newspapers, turning
The lights on or
Turning the lights
Off

It doesn't seem like
Much when its
10 hours before I have
To get up for work
And once I was
A boy of such
Promise

Railroad Boots Beside The Bed

Railroad boots beside the bed
And dreams and trains and endless mud
Down streets my grandfather walked
On his way to the paper mill
Back when my father was alive
And young and hopeful and the
Sky over the bay was full of ducks
And smoke. Back when my
Grandmother cut hair on
The second floor on 22'nd and Parade
Back when cousins became nuns
Or moved to Detroit or went to
College down state. Back when
My aunts and uncles married well
And everyone stayed in the church
Back when I had never sat in a room
Without a crucifix.

Back when childhood was a maggot
In the center or a chestnut. Back when
It was painful to want. Back when I
Pulled the parking break on the foot
Of State Street and the car started
Rolling down hill toward the dock.

Back when all of our parents were married.
Back when dust in the air meant
There were unending numbers of
Jobs. Back when girls wore
Saddle shoes and plaid jumpers.

Back when love was better than love.
Back when King Kong made me cry
Back when the neighbors were like family
Back when school was sad and boring
And everybody knew our family name but
Nobody knew me.
Back when winter time could kill.
Back when anyone's uncle would give you
A beer. Back when even the children
Got drunk at weddings.
Back when a polka was just your aunt
Dragging you around the dance floor
Back when Easter butter was sculpted
To look like the Lamb of God
Back when the stained glass windows
In each family's church
Had each family's name on them
Back when we buried our dead

In the same places
And we stood there with them
On holidays
Back when I knew my people
Like I knew my city.

Railroad boots beside the bed
And dreams and trains and
Endless mud…

Dress Rehearsal

Today on the street
I walked past a group of children
Playing funeral, laying
Daffodils on a young boy's chest
While he lay on the bottom step
Below the porch
Trying not to laugh
Holding his hands in mock rigor
Folded on his chest

The solemnity of death
Is something we must learn
And practice in a game
While we still have
One grandparent
Left

I stand behind the
Living children
Watching them
Place a flower
Step back
And pretend
To cry

Coyote In Workboots

I am coyote in work boots
Warping calluses onto my right hand
Scrubbing screens, beating my knuckles
Off wooden frames and breathing
Steam – in my head I am
Coyote in work boots
Tricking the hours for coin
Punching the clock 'till it bleeds
Turning mind games into production
Turning dreams into paychecks
Turning my best years into
Gone

Rent check, car insurance, the
Phone bill, the gas bill, the
Electric bill, a loan payment
Health insurance, union dues
Groceries and gasoline
Anti-depressants, pain pills, Lipitor
And Losinipril – sometimes even
A Saturday night

I am coyote in work boots
I am raven on a fork lift

I am the trick, trick, trickiest
Trick turning towards the
Hot face of the furnace
Or the sharp wheels of
A train hauling coal and
Shipping parts, moving earth
And pushing the sky at Heaven
One lived life at a time

I am coyote in work boots
I am strait time, over time,
Time and a half, mandatory overtime
Six days a week, nine month
Contract employee with
A summer job in a print shop
For half the wages and no
Health insurance, three months
When I am only half a man

Drunk on vodka and tap water
With high blood pressure and an
Ex-wife, three daughters, child
Support, an ex-girlfriend with
Drug problems and a live with

Woman who looks at me like
I am as beautiful as star light

I am coyote in work boots
Ancient and wise but disguised
As a working class, holy fool
Dented flesh, depressed and
Self medicating in a rented room
Writing poetry, talking shit
Taking meds and setting alarms
So I can get up in time to
Do it all again

I am coyote in work boots
A trickster, playing hysterical
Tricks on myself for
Reasons I don't understand

When John Henry Went To College

The Swannanoa tunnel
Coughed up its dead
To gerrymander the Ashville
City council, de-gentrification
Was called for and the rain
Needed a working class
To fall on

John Henry went to
The company store
Applied for a Pell grant
And borrowed sixty thousand
Dollars for a bachelor's degree
In philosophy – even the hammer
Told him he was wrong

"What are you gonna do
With a degree in philosophy"
The hammer demanded

"I want to think deep thoughts"
John Henry cried.
"Deep as the mines, deep as the tunnels
Through Blue Ridge

I want to study the meaning
Of life from a socialist perspective
So I can pin point the source
Of my angst and situate it between
Capitalist exploitation and the
Failure of the existential design
I want to challenge the myth of
The Nietcheian superman
As the driving force of history
And find my meaning in the
Social forces that put
That little piece of steel
In my tiny hand when I was
A child

"You just want to blame me"
The hammer said

"I want to study religion
I want to know Allah and Buddha
And Moses. I want to know Plato's
Unmoved mover. I want Darwin and
Physics and the Big Bang
I want a better explanation of
The universe than the one I learned
At the dinner table"

"You think you're better than me"
The hammer raged

John Henry and the hammer
Argued like this for
The next four years
John came home less and less
The hammer stopped giving him money
The holidays were tense

But the hammer was proud of John
And on graduation day
He sat in the 47'th row and
Clapped until his hands went numb
He hugged John in front
Of the whole family
And let him come home
Giving him the whole summer
To put that degree
To use

Come the fall the rain fell
On the working class
The student loan starts coming due
And he owed his soul
To the company store

Now, this aint the story
Of George Santayana and
This aint the story of
Harold Bloom – this is
The story of John Henry

So he puts that diploma
In his sock draw and he
Picks up that hammer and
A little piece of steel
And, as everybody knows
He eventually dies
With that hammer
In his hands

Ink Stained Ghost

My shop rags can stand up without
Me in them, – my ink stained ghost
Leaning on a plastic Virgin Mary
Behind our sunflowers – the laces
From my work boots tied together
Make a four foot fuse to the torn
Cuff of the jeans I wore every day
For three and a half months – me, in
Effigy – my ink stained ghost – the
Scarecrow meant to warn away
The scavengers and the neighborhood
Children from this kind of work and
This kind of life – the shadow of
One half of a co-dependant relationship
That uses alcohol to numb the pain
Of our inability to end it clean
Go our separate ways and let our
Lives get better – the caricature
Of my Polish grandfather, who went
Back to the paper mill after his
First stroke because he pitched
For the shop baseball team and there
Was talk that they might get to play
The Yankees – the family resemblance

To my father toiling six days a week
Since before I was born ton the day
The cancer took him—the bag of wind
Who muttered about revolution just
Under his breath while up to his eye
Balls in shit work every day for three
And a half months—the peasant who
Is more afraid to be without work than
He is of the work that drove his blood
Pressure towards maintenance medication
And divorce and cirrhosis of the liver –
The fool who can't change his life and
Can't figure out why his life won't
Change – the boy who wanted to
Grow up to be John Henry and Phil
Ochs, who became the worst of both
The fatal heart attach and the suicide
By hanging – the man who can't look
Into his own eyes in the bathroom mirror
At work – the ink stained ghost in
The garden outside my back door that
Goes up in flames tonight as I raise
A glass of vodka and tap water to
Toast my last day at the print shop

Bottom Shelf Vodka And A Love That Will Last Forever
For Janice

Working class, working poor
And a love that works as hard as we do
Living on tap water and steamed salmon
Lying on a bed of stir fried garlic
And cabbage – middle aged now
And finding hope in a dingy efficiency
Apartment on the lower west side
We are a genteel poverty with
Bicycles in the kitchen and two cats
In the driveway side window
With her three jobs to my two
And not an unpaid bill in four years
We are the evidence of things unseen
Holding hands in the save a lot
And speaking sweetly in line
At the country fair, buying a salad
And a six inch smart turkey sub
When I tell her to get anything
She wants and she says
"See, I'm a cheap date"
The counter girl says
"You're so cute I hope I
Find something like that"
And I am not making this up

We are a perfect fit
We are the American dream
We are grace under fire
Attending four funerals for
Every wedding, rushing to hospitals
And missing work to take care
Of each other through illness
We are reasonable expectations
And answered prayers
Washing our clothes in the bath tub
Buying clothes at the Salvation Army
We are an elegant balance
A moon and a planet in orbit
With gravity hands touching
Each other's light and water
We are both divorced and well past
Our prime, finding each other
In a cruel and unforgiving world
Where people live in fear
And people die alone
We are perfect
Like bottom shelf vodka
And a love that will
Last forever

About the Author

Mark Borczon has spent the last thirty years working for the Office for Students with Disabilities at Edinboro University of Pennsylvania. He grew up in Erie Pennsylvania. Spent many years dreaming and roaming the streets. Started writing poems in the eighties. Published some in the 'zine great nineties. Trying to learn his way into the online world of words. He is fifty two years old.

Nixes Mate Books features small-batch artisanal literature, created by writers that use all 26 letters of the alphabet and then some, honing their craft the time-honored way: one line at a time.

Other or Forthcoming Nixes Mate titles:
WE ARE PROCESSION, SEISMOGRAPH | Devon Balwit
ON BROAD SOUND | Rusty Barnes
JESUS IN THE GHOST ROOM | Rusty Barnes
CAPP ROAD | Matt Borczon
THE WILLOW HOWL | Lisa Brognano
A WORLD WHERE | Paul Brookes
SHE NEEDS THAT EDGE | Paul Brookes
SQUALL LINE ON THE HORIZON | Pris Campbell
MY SOUTHERN CHILDHOOD | Pris Campbell
A FIRE WITHOUT LIGHT | Darren C. Demaree
LABOR | Lisa DeSiro
KINKY KEEPS THE HOUSE CLEAN | Mari Deweese
AIR & OTHER STORIES | Lauren Leja
HITCHHIKING BEATITUDES | Michael McInnis
SMOKEY OF THE MIGRAINES | Michael McInnis
THE LIVES OF ATOMS | Lee Okan
LUBBOCK ELECTRIC | Anne Elezabeth Pluto
STARLAND | Jessica Purdy
WAITING FOR AN ANSWER | Heather Sullivan
COMES TO THIS | Jeff Weddle
HEART OF THE BROKEN WORLD | Jeff Weddle
NIXES MATE REVIEW ANTHOLOGY 2016/17

nixesmate.pub/books